DRONFIELD
& DISTRICT

BRITAIN IN OLD PHOTOGRAPHS

DRONFIELD
& DISTRICT

ROGER REDFERN

SUTTON PUBLISHING LIMITED

Sutton Publishing Limited
Phoenix Mill · Thrupp · Stroud
Gloucestershire · GL5 2BU

First published 1999

Copyright © Roger Redfern, 1999

Title page photograph: The Peel Monument,
High Street, 1890s.

British Library Cataloguing in Publication Data
A catalogue record for this book is available from the
British Library.

ISBN 0-7509-2395-4

Typeset in 10.5/13.5 Photina.
Typesetting and origination by
Sutton Publishing Limited.
Printed in Great Britain by
Ebenezer Baylis, Worcester.

CONTENTS

A high-angled viewpoint at the heart of old Dronfield town, *c.* 1965. Taken by the district's best-known post-war photographer, E. Hector Kyme, it shows the Peel Monument, Blue Stoops Inn and parish church on a quiet Sunday morning. Hector was not slow to grasp an opportunity for an unusual photograph: seeing the scaffolding on the gable-end of Manor Villas he climbed quickly to the chimney-stack and pressed the shutter (see also page 17).

INTRODUCTION

In a strange sort of way the old market town–turned industrial centre–cum dormitory doesn't quite know which way to look. It lies on the extreme northern boundary of Derbyshire, hard against Sheffield's southern edge. In fact, the neighbouring villages of Dore, Totley and Norton were transferred to the city of Sheffield in 1934 and there have been other small boundary changes over the years. Some residents look mainly to Sheffield; others are Derbyshire orientated.

No matter whether one considers the Dronfield district (including, too, Coal Aston, Dronfield Woodhouse, Holmesfield and Barlow) as an adjunct to Sheffield or firmly part of Derbyshire territory it has its own special character and I hope this assemblage of photographs will convince you. With one exception they were all taken in the twentieth century, many by that well-known and well-loved Dronfield personality E. Hector Kyme.

Samuel Bagshaw called the place 'a large, ancient village, pleasantly situated in a romantic valley on the Chesterfield road' in 1846. At that time there were 417 houses and a population of 1,986 inhabitants. That romantic valley was soon to be desecrated by an increase in the number of collieries and an expansion of the iron and steel industry alongside the arrival of the Midland Railway's main line in 1870.

Dronfield and district had been a cradle of the edge tool industry with a long pedigree of scythe, sickle and spade makers working from small, valley-bottom factories. Through the nineteenth century large-scale expansion brought highs and lows of employment, and the generation of much air pollution.

With the demise of most of this manufacture since the Second World War the district has become a much cleaner place. The development of huge housing estates on both sides of the Drone Valley has transformed Dronfield from a well-balanced, workaday town of intimate scale to nothing much more than a straggling dormitory for outsiders with little affinity or affection for the long heritage here.

I hope that these photographs will give newcomers an impression of what they've missed, and oldtimers some happy memories of the people and places associated with the old town and its rural frame.

Machin's Yard, Soaper Lane, nearing the end, on a June day in 1959. This fine old property was a lovely hotchpotch of stone at the back of the early nineteenth-century Beech House. It lay empty for several years before being demolished and replaced by Machin's Court.

CHAPTER ONE

DRONFIELD

Dronfield's ancient High Street at the end of the Second World War. Few cars troubled pedestrians in those days; most folk seemed to walk down the middle of the road. On the left are the remnants of Mrs Bennett's sweet shop, while on the right is the grand old façade of Hall Farmhouse where the Tomlinsons lived until it was needlessly destroyed in the 1950s. Out of sight on the extreme right is Ron Fisher's house, now the Samad Indian Restaurant.

The familiar façade of Dronfield's Manor House at the end of the nineteenth century. Dronfield was a royal demesne in 1086 and passed through several families until purchased by John Rotherham in 1749. It later passed by gift to Joseph Cecil and much of old Dronfield remained part of the Cecil estates until the middle of the twentieth century. Notice the young monkey puzzle tree in the central bed, well remembered by older residents and removed relatively recently.

In 1939 Mrs Rotherham Cecil moved from the Manor House to Rossington House, Stubley Lane, and the Manor House became Dronfield's Public Library and Council Offices. Here we see the well-grown monkey puzzle on a bright summer morning, c. 1950.

A meet of the Barlow Hounds in the town's High Street caused no traffic congestion, *c.* 1905. Notice that the Manor House was still surrounded by a high stone wall. Major William Wilson of Horsleygate is mounted on the left.

A January night in the Manor House grounds, looking to Manor Villas (centre) and the Old Manor House (right) at the top of High Street, *c.* 1950. The high stone wall surrounding the grounds had not yet been removed.

Manor House revealed! The Peel Monument in the town's High Street with the stone wall recently removed from the town's library grounds. The removal of the three great chimney-stacks from the Manor House roof did nothing to enhance the balance of this fine early eighteenth-century house. Did the surrounding wall's removal improve the aesthetic appeal of this part of the old town?

The Peel Monument was erected in about 1850 to commemorate the Repeal of the hated Corn Laws in 1848. It is a foggy autumn evening, the sort of conditions that E. Hector Kyme loved to treat as a challenge as he set up his camera and tripod for a tricky long exposure!

Mr May, Manor House caretaker, at work in the front garden, late 1950s. The high garden wall had now been removed, allowing this photograph to be taken from High Street. On the horizon is the great horse chestnut tree on the Finney Fields that was felled during construction of the Unstone–Dronfield bypass.

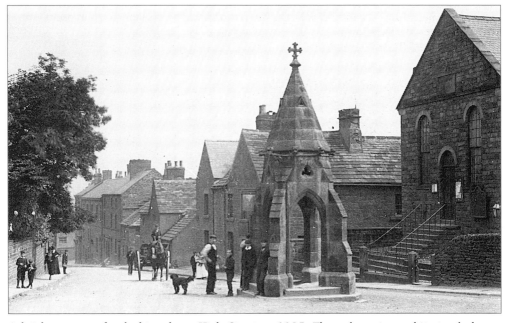

A bright summer day looking down High Street, c. 1905. The only major architectural change since that time has been the demolition of Mrs Bennett's sweet shop beyond the Blue Stoops Inn, now a car park. Children and men always spent spare time sitting or standing at the Peel Monument – until the local population moved from the nearby old world housing to council estates at the edge of town.

From an attic window at The Cottage overlooking High Street on a January afternoon in 1956 we see beyond the Peel Monument (still sporting finial decoration put there for the Coronation of the Queen in 1953) to the top of Farwater Lane. What a difference today! Gone are 'Tiptoe' Mitchell's cobbler's shop, Mr Davidson's cottage and all the fine stone properties in Farwater Lane and Eldon Croft, replaced by the tasteless bleakness of the Civic Centre.

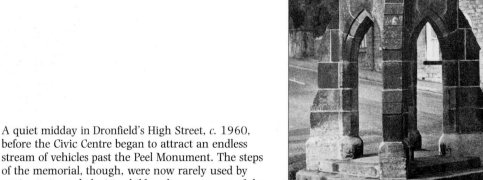

A quiet midday in Dronfield's High Street, *c.* 1960, before the Civic Centre began to attract an endless stream of vehicles past the Peel Monument. The steps of the memorial, though, were now rarely used by resting men and playing children because most of the nearby cottages had already been demolished.

The Elizabethan Old Manor House stands in what was known as Talbot's Yard near the top of High Street. Originally a yeoman farmer's dwelling, it lay unoccupied for many years in the middle of the twentieth century.

The east front of the Old Manor House in Talbot's Yard, 1971. It was used by the town council for many years as their Building Department's store, hence the stack of bricks seen here. An early hand-propelled fire brigade pump and ladders stood forgotten in a corner of the yard throughout the Second World War. The old house was subsequently restored for habitation and is now called Rookery Cottage.

From Rookery Cottage near the top of High Street, this is the eastward view over garden walls to The Cottage, Dronfield Hall and the parish church. The Cottage, once owned by Lord Byron and used as a Dame School, is a 1622 addition to an older rear wing; Dronfield Hall is an early eighteenth-century house, for many years the home and surgery of the well-remembered Dr George Clifton.

E. Hector Kyme was always quick to spot an opportunity. On this bright Sunday morning in the mid-1960s he was soon up a ladder and taking photographs from scaffolding on Manor Villas. While he took this view of the Peel Monument, Methodist Free Church and parish church (above) I took a photograph of him in action from my bedroom window (below).

In this photograph taken by Kyme from the steps of the Methodist Free Church in 1967 we are looking nort
across High Street to The Cottage. The Victorian bay windows were added to the ground floor soon after Jarv
Smedley and his family moved there in 1861. Dronfield's first stationmaster, George Poplar, was appointed whe
the Midland arrived in 1870 and he married the Smedleys' daughter Emily in 1872. The family stayed at Th
Cottage until 1913.

he Methodist Free Church, High Street, was one of the town's largest chapels, built in 1863. This photograph
ates from about 1905 and shows chapel members at the annual Feast celebration. To the left of the banner
owler hat) is Lawrence Gould, well remembered as proprietor of High Street's fish and chip shop (top part of the
resent Manor Hotel); to the right of the banner (bowler hat, wing collar and tie) is Walter Leek who lived with
is wife at the bottom of Farwater Lane and sold vegetables and young plants from his market garden. Few, if any,
f those looking at the camera on that happy day are now alive.

This pre-1929 photograph shows members of Harry Hardwick's celebrated choir at a musical presentation in the Congregational Chapel, Lea Road. Among those ranged at high level along the back are Ernest Burton, Alfred Dunham, Frank Elliott, Fred Booker, Frank Silcock and Herbert Hardwick. In the top row of ladies are Florrie Redfern, Nora Havenhand and Edith Hardwick; in the row below them are the Principals – Charlie Scholey, Helen Talbot, Ethel Chapman, Stanley Beckett and Lizzie Havenhand. The bottom complete row of ladies is, left to right, Lily Levick, Emily Sharp, Edith Shirt, Joyce Bingham, -?-, Connie Shelton, Minnie Webster, Annie Havenhand, Minnie Simpson, Edith Kyme, Mrs John Haslam and George Dundas. On the front row are John Parr (oboe), Miss Hawkins (violin), Alice Hindle (violin), Cyril Baxby (violin), Harry Baxby, Mrs Rotherham Cecil, Harry Hardwick (conductor) and Stanley Holmes (trombone).

The Feast procession assembles on Wreakes Lane, 26 June 1906. In the background is the funfair which has just arrived in town to provide the highlight of the year for many of Dronfield's young people.

The town's first motor fire engine outside The Rookery (now the site of Jowitt's car park, Wreakes Lane), c. 1911. Though the fire station was at Sheffield Road at this time the new engine was photographed outside the north front of Captain Skinner's large house. The brigade is, left to right, H. Allen, C.C. Wood, Captain W.W. Skinner, F. Hannam, H. Green, W. Rawson, J. Roe and D. Browse.

The last occupants of The Rookery were Mr and Mrs Jim Savage and their family. Here we see them in th enclosed garden on the south side of the house with their grandchildren Niggy, Peter and Marguerita, *c.* 1957.

Opposite: The grounds of The Rookery looking north towards Wreakes Lane, 1966. Already bulldozers ar preparing the site for Jowitt's works; happily the mature maple and beech trees in the foreground have bee preserved. Note the leather front seats from Jim Savage's scrapped Jaguar car at the foot of the maple tree!

The Rookery, nearing the end. After the Savage family retired to Mousehole, Cornwall, in the early 1960s this fine house was purchased by Messrs Jowitt and stood empty until demolished in the mid-1960s. The oldest part of the house (right) dated from the seventeenth century and should have been listed and preserved: at least the art deco bathroom suite was rescued and removed to the author's home!

View down Farwater Lane from the entrance to Eldon Croft, *c.* 1900. The gabled Elizabethan building is the Mason's Arms Inn. After it was closed in the 1930s the licence was transferred to the new public house of the same name at the end of Cemetery Road. Had this ensemble of old buildings been in the Yorkshire Dales or the Cotswolds it would have been saved and restored. The first cottage (left) stood in the same position as the present Yorkshire Building Society office.

The bottom of Farwater Lane on a sunny morning in the late winter of 1955. E. Hector Kyme has set up his camera and tripod and, using delayed action, poses in the foreground.

Almost the same viewpoint as the picture above but a year earlier. The photographer's children, Sheila and Andrew, snowball in front of the attractive old cottages that were eventually swept away to give access to the Civic Centre's rear car park.

The town's monstrous, tasteless Civic Centre that replaced the delights of sylvan Eldon Croft in 1970.

Another view of the new Civic Centre, *c.* 1972. Using a tripod and delayed action, E. Hector Kyme (left) and his dog Robbie greet a friend where Mr Dent used to grow vegetables and young plants for sale, all in a sea of surrounding lupins.

The town's new Civic Hall and Health Centre, 1971. Notice the original entrance to the car park, before the range of shops was built in the right foreground. This hideous Civic Hall was demolished in 1999 to make way for a more substantial replacement – not before time!

The first homes of the mighty Gosforth Valley development were built in 1966 at Summer Green, adjacent to the junction of Gomersall Lane and Farwater Lane (later renamed Gosforth Lane). Here we are at Garth Way, looking over the Drone Valley and the town to the Coal Aston ridge and new Holmesdale housing estate, c. 1968.

The Lea Brook, draining the Gosforth Valley, had long been a dumping ground in the town. In 1971 E. Hecto
Kyme took it upon himself to clean up what is essentially an attractive 'green lung'. He rallied a group of lad
from his Sheffield school (Newfield) and they set to on a summer Saturday to lift this lot from the stream's bec
E.H.K. and Robbie are on the left: a tripod and delayed action in use again.

n another weekend in the same summer a second team continued the clean-up, filling skips provided by the uncil. Among those seen here are Ron Hepworth (left), E.H.K. and Robbie, Alan Herring and Ian Cottier, deputy admaster at Henry Fanshawe School (right, with beard). Behind them are the cottages in The Knot and onfield Primary School.

This view of about 1910 is still recognizable – looking down the steep path at Fanshawe Bank towards the Lea Brook where it passes close to the Bath House, below the parish church.

Frosty evening, Fanshawe Bank, 1958.

The Chantry is an early nineteenth-century house built on to the south side of the Green Dragon Inn, and takes its name from the chantry house or priests' dwelling associated with Beauchief Abbey and Dronfield parish church. This chantry house was eventually converted into the public house in the sixteenth century, but the builder of The Chantry used the association to name his house.

The floodlit Chantry on a cold winter evening in the 1960s. This was the home of Herbert Noel Lucas, solicitor and member of the local iron-founding family firm until his death in 1924. It later became the home and surgery of Dr J. Wilson, and is today the Chantry Hotel and home of the celebrated Roy and Jackie Toaduff.

In the late 1790s J.M.W. Turner was tramping the country for his publishers, making drawings of buildings and townscapes for book illustrations. These sketchbooks are now in the National Gallery collection and include subjects in Derbyshire and Yorkshire. In addition to sketches of Sheffield from Meersbrook there is this one of Dronfield's parish church from the banks of one of the town's mill ponds, now close to the site of the railway station. Vale House is conspicuous to the left.

Vale House, though adjacent to Lea Road and Church Street, is something of a secret building with its sunk garden surrounded by high walls. Like The Chantry and Rose Hill it was formerly a home of the numerous Luc family. Remarkably unchanged since J.M.W. Turner's drawing over two centuries ago, the chimney-stacks a easily recognizable in his sketch.

winter night at the heart of the old town. The Red House of 1731 (left), The Grange and the Old Grammar
chool (right) stand quiet under January snow over forty years ago.

homas Fanshawe was responsible for getting a new
choolhouse built in about 1579 under the terms of
s uncle Henry Fanshawe's will. This building
verlooks Fanshawe Bank, and after the school moved
 the floor of the Drone Valley in 1867 the old
uilding was almost entirely rebuilt externally. Even
day, though, exposed stones inside the house bear
ites and initials scratched by pupils up to four
nturies ago.

Another snowy night, *c.* 1965: this time a view through the parish church lych gate to the Green Dragon In beyond Church Street.

The Green Dragon Inn, Church Street, is one of the town's most historic buildings. It contains the fabric, much altered, of the original chantry house or priests' dwelling and the Lords' brewhouse at the rear. It became a public house soon after 1545 when a second floor was inserted in the hall.

The parish church of St John the Baptist from the south-east with the former Congregational Chapel (left), *c.* 1950. The new fall of snow picks out the roof of the long gone Red Lion Inn (centre) at the bottom of Church Street, where the well-remembered Mrs Sykes was landlady for so many years.

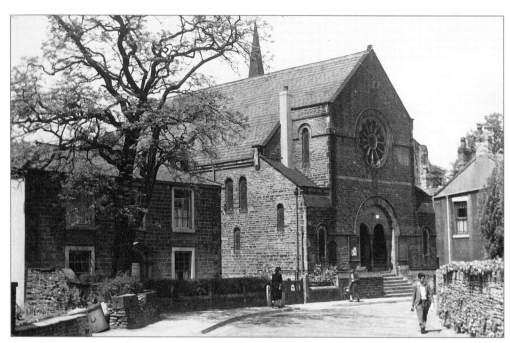

Looking along Lea Road, spring 1950. The Congregational Chapel dominates the picture, with the Manse and its false acacia tree (*robinia pseudoacacia*) (left) and the gable end of the Red Lion Inn (right). Walking towards us on the pavement is Miss Bessie Bedingfield; she and her sister Edith were the district's joint Registrar of Births and Deaths. They were the daughters of Waller King Bedingfield, headmaster of the Grammar School (1869–88).

The south side of the parish church from the Primary School, School Lane, on a summer day in 1950. The most interesting features here are the grand old farmhouse of Buttermere Farm (left) attached to the long cruck barn alongside Church Street. Adjacent to it (extreme left) is the gable end of the brick house where Jack Fletcher ('Clip and Nudge') operated as a hairdresser. Both these houses were sadly demolished to spoil this part of Church Street's architectural unity. A car park occupies their sites today.

Opposite: Looking in the opposite direction along Lea Road to the junction with School Lane. The classical proportions of Williams and Glyn's Bank (now the Royal Bank of Scotland) remain unaltered from the opening day, 28 June 1873. At that time it was a branch of the Sheffield and Rotherham Joint Stock Banking Company, open on Wednesday and Saturday from 11 am to 4 pm under the supervision of a local agent, Hugh Garside Rhodes. It was the first bank to open in Dronfield, largely prompted by the opening in the same year of Wilson, Cammell & Co.'s large integrated steel works on Callywhite Lane.

Work in progress on the 132 ft spire of the parish church, early 1950s. Here, again, Buttermere Farm and Jack Fletcher's house are seen to advantage from the grounds of the Primary School.

Winter night, Church Street, from the grounds of The Grange, *c.* 1955. We are looking due east to the rear of the Green Dragon Inn and The Chantry (right).

Remnants of snowfall on the dilapidated walls behind the present Manor Hotel, High Street, January 1967: The Red House (left), The Grange and the Old Grammar School (right).

Another winter's day, this time in February 1951. Buttermere Farm and its cruck barn are a brilliant foreground for the parish church as seen from the Primary School grounds. Note the distant chimney of Lucas's 'Bottom Yard' works (right of church).

pring sundown from Snape Hill Lane, 1950. The Vicarage (now the Old Rectory) stands above Soaper Lane.

he ancient south porch of the parish church, 1900. The
tone coffin that adorns the corner on the right
owadays was not in place at this time. Such coffins were
nly provided for important people like the Rector or Lord
f the Manor.

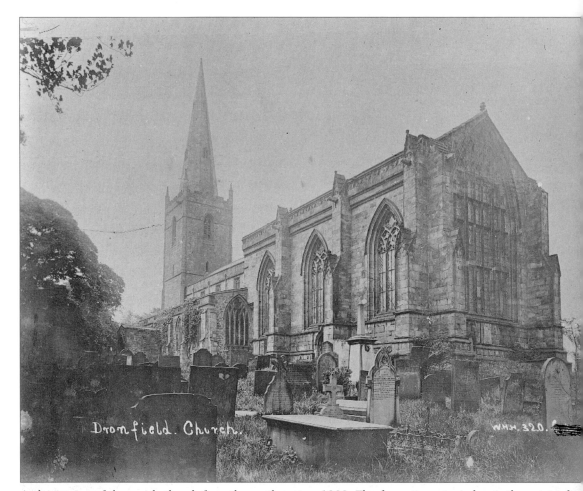

Dronfield. Church.

W.H.H. 320.

A classic view of the parish church from the south-east, *c.* 1900. The dramatic east window is the outstandin feature of the church. Originally filled with stained glass it fell into serious dilapidation after the surrender c Beauchief Abbey in 1537. The east window actually fell out before 1563 and crows were nesting in the chance Note the absence of a church clock, only fitted in the tower in 1904.

The nave of the parish church looking west from the chancel arch. The wonderful black oak pulpit carved with Tudor designs is on the right.

A detail of the present east window of the parish church, showing Abraham about to sacrifice his son Isaac.

The carved creatures on the choir stalls are some of the finest in any country church. The oldest parts of these stalls date from the fifteenth century.

The magnificent modern reredos and high altar of the parish church were carved by Advent Hunstone of Tideswell and placed here in 1907. Here we see the front of the altar, showing the crucified Christ being placed in the tomb.

The parish church Ladies Day Outing to the Peak District, 1938. Back row, left to right: -?-, bus driver, Mrs Staniforth, -?-, Mrs Elsie Watson, Mrs Emmott, Mrs Mullins, Mrs Triphena Mathewman, Miss Doris Harrison, Mrs P. Grocutt, Mrs Taylor, Mrs Harrison, Mrs Mullins, -?-, -?-, Mrs Ward, Mrs Parkes, Mrs Dean, Mrs Ward, Mrs Tyrrell. Seated: Mrs Corker, Mrs G.E. Pashley, Miss Beswick, Mrs Rhodes, Mrs Truswell, John Emmott, Mrs Margaret Jennings, Barbara Ward, -?-, Miss Muriel Hodgson, Mrs Bingham, Mrs Fred Ward, Mrs Windle, Miss Gladys Grocutt.

Dronfield Girl Guides await their train at the town's railway station en route for summer camp, late 1930s. The tall figure (back left) is Miss Beatrice Lucas of Rose Hill, Princess Road.

Dronfield Rangers put on a production of *The Taming of the Shrew* in the 1930s. Left to right: Hilda Higginbottom, -?-, Muriel Young, Kitty Redhead, Dorothy Allen, -?-, Grace Hoy.

Girls at Dronfield Primary School, School Lane, who had recently won scholarships to the Grammar School, 1930s. Back row, left to right (Minor scholars): Wendy Thomas, Betty Draycott, Mildred Brusell. Front row (Foundation scholars): Iris Bartram, Gladys Butcher, Audrey Dunham, Dorothy Bargh, Audrey Tomlinson, Peggy Scothern.

Staff, student teachers and senior pupils at Dronfield Council School, School Lane, *c.* 1910. Standing: sixth from left: Maynard Ward; tenth from left: Miss White; eleventh from left: Mr Taylor; extreme right: Mrs Alsibrook. Seated: third from left: Miss Outram; fourth from left: Mr Gledhill (Headmaster); fifth from left: Miss Taylor.

Dronfield Council School Vegetable Show, August 1917. Produce competing for prizes certainly had the tables groaning on this day during the First World War. There was, of course, a great drive to produce as much home-grown food as possible at this time. On the right is Maynard Ward, a teacher at the school for many years.

Dronfield Infants School, September 1932. Miss Taylor was by this time headmistress. The girls would be seven or eight year olds, with younger brothers and sisters included in the photograph. Back row, left to right: Muriel Austin, Iris Barton, Joan Belton, -?-, Miriam Atkin, -?-, -?-, -?-, -?-, -?-, -?-, Kathleen Wood. Third row: Joyce Bird, Joyce Wainwright, Eileen Bennett, Annie Lomas, -?-, -?-, Margaret Gibson, -?-, Jean Sutton, Mary Gregory, -?-. Second row: -?-, Annie Gregory, Joan Redhead, Vera Dickens, Joyce Liversidge, Marjorie Brothwell, Averil Thomas, Barbara Jessop, -?-, Marian Bracewell. Front row: -?-, Joyce Pearson, Winnie Ingham, ? Preston, -?-, -?-, Maynard Holmes, Eric Jordan, Joan Liversidge, Joan Briggs, ? Walker, Verna Redhead.

A group of Dronfield girls at Amber Valley Camp near Ashover, May 1954. Included in the back row are Margaret Lamb, Mary Nash, Judith Pound and Carol Howson. In the second row are Jean Austen and Joan Maisfield. In the third row are Hazel Platts and Doreen Freebre. The fourth row includes Ann Wilkes and Betty Whitaker. In the front row are Wendy Bell and Peggy Rawson.

Dronfield Council School Sports Day prize giving on the field at School Lane, *c.* 1952. Mrs Rotherham Cecil presents Andrew Kyme with a prize. Also in the picture are Ernest Harris (with paper), Mrs D. Mahon (school secretary), George Brewin (with pipe) and Headmaster Jack Hewitson.

Dronfield Scout troop at the edge of the Grammar School field, *c.* 1905. On the left is the large greenhouse (the Headmaster, Charles Chapman Baggaley (1888–1926) was a keen gardener), beyond is the science block (built 1893) and the original school building and Headmaster's house (built 1866).

The imposing neo-Elizabethan south front of Dronfield Grammar School, 1930. It was built in 1866 when the school moved here from the original school site at Fanshawe Bank.

The Grammar School's Memorial Garden was constructed in 1950 to the memory of old pupils killed during the Second World War. This photograph was taken in the summer of 1951.

Soon after Messrs Clifford Proctor had completed work on the Memorial Garden, 1950. The clock on the wall behind was part of the new memorial. Left to right: Miss Riggs, Miss Webley, Mrs Millican, Mr Millican (Headmaster) and Miss Doreen Darley.

The pond at the centre of Dronfield Grammar School's Memorial Garden, soon after completion in 1950. The garden was opened and the clock unveiled by Brigadier G.H. Fanshawe on 5 June 1950.

New Hall, Chesterfield Road, is an early Victorian house and now the oldest part of the Dronfield School. It was formerly the home of the Hall family who ran a timber merchants' business from the yard behind. It was originally built by William Tofield as a present for his daughter, whose initials can still be seen on the wrought-iron banisters. The well-known crocuses were already blooming under the weeping ash tree in the front garden when Mrs Emily Browes went to live there in 1890, as a child-companion to Tofield's widowed daughter. She is seen here at the front door in about 1900.

An overturned bunsen burner used to keep the frost off an oil engine caused a fire which destroyed the outbuildings used in the timber business in February 1919. Mr Hall never fully recovered from the shock and walked along the railway line towards Unstone in May 1920, only to be killed by a southbound train.

It was purchased by the Governors of Dronfield Grammar School in 1927 and was the Headmaster's home during the entire tenure of Norman S. Millican. From 1953 it has been used as school accommodation.

Rose Hill overlooks Chesterfield Road but is approached from Princess Road (formerly Princess Street but changed between the wars when residents aspired to a more upmarket address). Though dated 1719 it has the countenance of half a century earlier, like neighbouring Chiverton House. For a long period in the twentieth century it was the home of the Lucas family. This photograph was taken on a January day in 1970.

Chiverton House, Chesterfield Road, was built in 1712 on the foundations of a much older mansion and, like Rose Hill, is in an architectural style by then well out of date. This, of course, adds to its fascination and greater charm. Probably built, again like Rose Hill, as the home of a wealthy lead merchant, it once was owned by the Dukes of Newcastle. It has been the home of the Rhodes family, mine owners, throughout the twentieth century.

Dronfield is the cradle
of the British edge tool
and malleable iron
industry. Not much
remains of this once
thriving valley bottom
activity but on this
particular winter
morning in the 1950s
trade remained brisk.
We are standing on
Paper Lane Bridge,
looking south over
Messrs Edward Lucas's
'Bottom Yard' works.

The same works on a
miserable January
morning, looking along
Chesterfield Road from
the bottom of Snape
Hill Lane, c. 1968.

The workforce at Messrs Edward Lucas's 'Bottom Yard' works, *c.* 1900. The Bridge Inn stands behind (left), and older readers will remember the wall of vertical railway sleepers that formed the boundary with the end of Lea Road.

The new motor trolley replaced man and horse power at the 'Bottom Yard' after the Second World War. Here we see moulders and oven workers with their new machine. Left to right: Ernest Grocutt ('Dobbin'), Fred Fearn (driver), Len Baxby, Harold Ward, Albert Webb and Harold Kay.

Core makers at the 'Bottom Yard' after the Second World War. Left to right: Maggie Vaughan (Apperknowle), Mary Fearn, Margaret Vaughan (Apperknowle), Dorothy Heeley (Unstone) and Sylvia Travis (Unstone).

When the 'Bottom Yard' works of Messrs Edward Lucas was finally demolished in the 1970s the original entrance arch was preserved as a monument to the first place in the world where malleable iron castings were made, in 1790.

The annual Cycle Parade procession passes Dronfield railway station, 1920s. This was one of the social highlights of the town's year.

Twenty years later part of the Cycle Parade procession assembles in Cliffe Park, with a local manufacturer's lorry carrying a tableau that includes 'Old Mother Riley'.

With the development of large housing
estates by Sheffield City Council at Lowedges
and Batemoor heavy rain brought quick
run-off and swollen headstreams of the River
Drone where previously fields had acted as a
sponge. A series of floods affected low-lying
parts of Dronfield in the 1950s and here we
see one such occasion at the junction of
Holmley Lane with Sheffield Road in 1958.
Mildred Joynes, John Taylor (on wall), Tony
Radford and a friend look on while young
Foster makes certain adjustments.

Virtually the same viewpoint, looking over the roadside wall to the flooded fields of Nether
Birchitt Farm.

The junction of Stubley Hollow with Sheffield Road used to be a large 'triangle' with the River Drone flowing in a deep hollow. Here a new culvert is being built in the 1960s prior to the entire hollow being filled in and a new road layout being created. Notice the old council yard where steam rollers were parked (top left), almost opposite the Coach and Horses Inn.

The old layout still exists at the junction of Stubley Hollow and Sheffield Road in the summer flood of 1958. The deep central hollow is filled by the swirling Drone and a laden lorry heads for Sheffield. Beyond, steam rollermen's mobile caravans stand in the old council yard.

Milking time on a spring morning at Nether Birchitt Farm, *c.* 1954. Jim Smith brings his herd in from the fields at the old farm opposite the Coach and Horses Inn, Sheffield Road. Note the old grindstones (bottom right), a remnant of Dronfield's historic edge tool manufacturing days.

Bleak midwinter at Nether Birchitt Farm. Jim Smith prepares to milk the cows in very different conditions from those in the previous picture.

High tide in Chesterfield Road! The River Drone has risen after heavy rain in the summer of 1958. The left-hand shop is now Dronfield Motor Spares, while the newsagent's is now the left-hand window and doorway of GT News.

A powerful torrent sweeps from the River Drone into Chesterfield Road on the same day in 1958. Everyone is confined to the pavement below the Grammar School wall.

Looking towards Chesterfield from the bottom of Green Lane on the same day in 1958. The signal box is still in position and operative near the south end of Dronfield's railway station.

The same view over thirty years earlier. This notorious bottleneck on the main road through the town caused several accidents, so the old Horse and Jockey Inn (right) was eventually demolished and the corner opened out. Since that time generations of local people have caught the bus to Sheffield at this place. On the left is Evans's greengrocer's shop, now the town's post office.

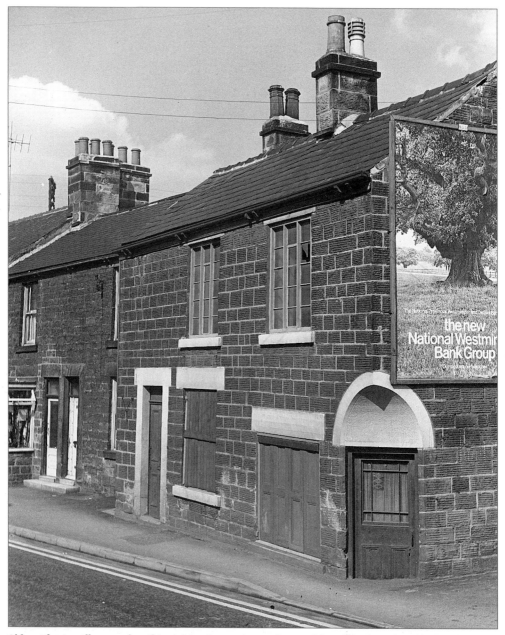

Old residents will remember this as Mrs Greaves's pot shop and hairdressing salon. This photograph was taken in 1970 when the building was awaiting demolition. To the left is Jackson's fish and chip shop (now a Chinese take-away) and beyond that the Old Sidings (formerly the Midland) Inn.

A grand period photograph, 1920s. Arthur Browes stands at the door of his grocer's shop adjacent to the town's Electra Palace cinema, Chesterfield Road. Born in 1882, Arthur Browes was a member of the parish church choir for sixty-seven years, dying in 1955 at the age of seventy-three. His wife, Emily (1886–1966), was a founder member of the parish church Mothers' Union.

A summer afternoon at Lea Road, *c.* 1947. Mrs Greaves (left), her daughter Eileen Haywood and grand-daughter, Arthur Browes, Audrey Browes and Mrs Emily Browes in the garden of the Browes's house.

The Fishers are an old Dronfield family whose different members have owned butchers' shops in various locations in the town. When William Fisher took delivery of his new van in 1926 its bodywork was finished at Rex Barker's garage (Mr Barker was also landlord of the White Swan Inn). Here is Rex Barker with that van at the bottom of Hallowes Lane – not the sort of place one would pose for a photograph today! The base of the town's War Memorial can be seen (top left) forty or so years before it was removed to the grounds of the Manor House, High Street. William Fisher's grandson, Frank, still operates the business from what may now be the oldest butcher's shop in the country, at the bottom of High Street.

Everything came to a stop at 2.45 p.m. on Sunday 29 October 1922 when the town's War Memorial was dedicated and unveiled at the bottom of Hallowes Lane. The unveiling was performed by Major General H.R. Davies CB (seen here in uniform). This memorial was designed by Old Whittington artist Joseph Siddall (1864–1942).

When the old Masons Arms Inn, Farwater Lane, was abandoned in the 1930s the licence was transferred to this new building at the junction of Chesterfield Road and Cemetery Road, seen here on a winter night, *c.* 1952.

The town's Feast procession going down Lea Road towards Hallowes Lane and Chesterfield Road, June 1928. Above: the author's mother and Aunt Mary stand on the pavement (extreme right) while Helen Silcock leans into the decorated dray. Below: Harry Haslam (trilby hat) and George Cartwright (cap) hold the banner of the Methodist Free Church.

Looking down Hallowes Lane towards Quoit Green, 1900. Despite appearances this section of road has changed little in a century. The width of the road is the same today but the glorious, leafy canopy has gone: Dutch Elm disease and a lack of interest in replacing lost trees have both played their part in removing the sylvan charm.

Dronfield's second car. Reuben Dearden's De Dion stands in the croft at Quoit Green House with the author's Uncle James (Dob) and Aunt Joan on board, *c.* 1905.

Another day in Quoit Green House's verdant croft, summer 1923. The author's Aunt Mary (standing) and mother, Rachel, play with Barrie.

In the garden at Quoit Green House, 1921. The two elder daughters of William Ward Barker – Annie Rhodes (1879–1947) (left) and Mary Dearden (1876–1947) – the author's great-aunt and grandmother respectively.

January snow, looking along Cemetery Road, 1926. The author's mother with Barrie, not long before new houses began to appear on the site of Brown's taxi cabin and neighbouring breeze block manufacturing business.

Hallowes Farm was built in 1657 by the Morewoods and remains one of the district's finest houses. Last farmed by the Johnsons, it became headquarters of the Hallowes Golf Club in 1925. Here's the north front, *c.* 1900.

The main door on the south front of the former Hallowes Farm, with the initials of the Morewood who built it in 1657.

A telephoto shot across the golf course to the south front of the Hallowes foreshortens the Coal Aston ridge behind, 1970. The high wall surrounding the front garden was removed in 1934 and the stone used to build the ballroom, seen here on the left.

An early post-war view from behind Ridgill's works, Callywhite Lane, shows Hallowes Rise, the nine 1930s houses beside Highgate Lane and the former Hallowes Farm in silhouette on the Hill Top skyline.

Another prospect from behind Ridgill's works, Callywhite Lane, c. 1946. This one is towards the south-west and shows Cemetery Road, Moorgate Crescent and Hallowes Lane (left), and the faint skyline of the Finney Fields (right).

Ridgill's works and Callywhite Lane on a wet day, *c.* 1948. By this time the works was called Mining Appliances Co.; the railway tracks are still in place in the foreground, lines that linked several factories with the main railway near Dronfield station.

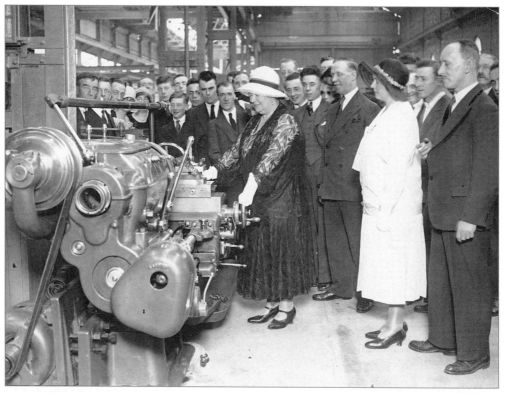

Mrs Ridgill operating a lathe at the opening ceremony of an extension at the family firm – Mining Appliances Co. – at Callywhite Lane, *c.* 1933. The works manager, Mr Hockey, stands extreme right and next to him are Helen Ridgill (the Ridgills' niece) and Mr Ridgill.

Celebration dinner on the same day in 1933. At the top table are Miss Holmes (left, cloche hat), Mr Haddon (behind, under King's portrait), Mr Hinds, Mrs Ridgill, Mr Ridgill, Helen Ridgill, Mr Hockey (works manager). On the right of the side table are Mr Hague (fourth from right), Fred Unwin (second from right) and Ron Unwin (extreme right).

The office block of Mining Appliances Co., Callywhite Lane, *c.* 1950. This is now part of P&V Ltd. The pair of villas still exists, much modified as offices.

A Bedford articulated lorry prepares to transport recent products of Mining Appliances Co., *c.* 1953.

Not a classic commercial vehicle rally but a view of the backyard of Mining Appliances Co. when used by the Kenning Motor Group, *c.* 1953.

Soaper Lane Bridge was unique for being a cast-iron structure supported by cast arches standing diagonally across the railway tracks. It had a maximum loading of 5 tons and is seen here being dismantled on Sunday 30 January 1977, to be replaced by a reinforced concrete arch.

Taken in 1974, this photograph shows the northern abutment of Soaper Lane Bridge, where the road passes over the railway tracks which, in turn, pass over the River Drone at the same point.

The cast-iron bridge of 1866 carrying the main Sheffield–Chesterfield railway tracks over the A61 trunk road in the middle of the town, 1955. This view shows the old wall and steps leading to The Cliffe at the junction of Green Lane with Callywhite Lane (behind the distant signpost) before major rebuilding.

The famous 'wooden bridge' linking Chesterfield Road with the 'stone bridge' carrying Lea Road over the railway. Generations of children have had nightmares of climbing this wooden structure as it slowly keeled over into the river below! Erected in about 1866, it is seen here in May 1955 – and looks much the same today.

Dronfield's so-called Castle was one of the
town's most enigmatic buildings, straddling
the River Drone upstream of Soaper Lane
Bridge. It was built in about 1790 and in
1871 it is known that a schoolteacher called
Mary Evans was living here. Ten years later
the Jennings family occupied it, together with
ten lodgers! The photograph below shows the
Castle in 1960, standing empty and derelict.
Soon afterwards the site was cleared.

Generations of railway enthusiasts used the lineside fence a short distance north of Soaper Lane Bridge. Here David Axe watches a north-bound freight train hauled by a Fowler 7F 0–8–0 on a grey day at the end of the Second World War.

Dronfield Colliery Sidings signal box stood opposite the 'spotters' fence', between Lucas's 'Tilt' works and the railway tracks. The kindly Mr Whitmore (seen here) used to allow enthusiasts to join him in the warm fug of the signal box and pull off signals under his instruction. When a bowler-hatted inspector was seen on an approaching locomotive footplate we ducked out of sight. This photograph was taken in 1948; that friendly box has long since passed into history.

The world's most famous locomotive – Class AI/3 No. 4472 *Flying Scotsman* – drifts light engine southwards towards Chesterfield, 1968. Having just passed under Wreakes Lane Bridge, it will soon echo through Dronfield station. At this date it was in the ownership of Alan Pegler and was fitted with two tenders to allow longer journeys, because of reduced opportunities to pick up coal and water.

Another day, same locomotive. No. 4472 *Flying Scotsman* thunders out of the south portal of Bradway Tunnel with a special train, October 1968. This picture was taken from the Drone aqueduct.

Naughty boys cross the aqueduct that carries the infant River Drone over the railway just south of Bradway Tunnel, February 1970. The intrepid pair are Peter Barnes and David Hodgson. The set of colour lights near the tunnel mouth indicate how the semaphore signals immediately outside the north portal were set.

Dronfield's Feast Parade passes up Green Lane soon after the Second World War. Messrs Riggott (left), Fox and Belton carry the Baptist Chapel Sunday School banner as the rest of the procession streams out of Cliffe Park's top entrance.

The author's grandfather Reuben Dearden with a friend in 'Parsley' Hall's 'rhubarb fields' at Green Lane, 1921. All this former farm land is now inundated with the bricks and mortar of the Holmesdale estate, developed after 1950.

Stonelow Road was pushed due east from Green Lane to connect up with Firthwood Road and Eckington Road in the 1960s. Here we see the newly built Stonelow Retirement Home (left), council flats and, beyond, Firth Wood rising to the skyline.

Dronfield's 'Model' Fire Brigade: entrants for the annual Cycle Parade just before the First World War assemble on Hartington Road. Left to right: Cyril Adlington, Willis Rawson, -?-, Mrs Adlington, Fred Talbot, Charlie Adlington, Albert Rawson, Fred Mundy.

An unidentified member of Dronfield's law enforcement unit poses in a yard behind Hartington Road houses, 1920s.

Cecil Road was one of the earliest to be developed off Snape Hill Lane in late Victorian times. On a midsummer's night we see the place where the road was extended in the late 1940s to develop the council estate behind. The Kyme family home stands on the left.

A view in the opposite direction at the opposite time of year: a view down Cecil Road at dusk on a January day in 1973.

The new fall of snow remains on the following morning: a sky heavy with more snow hangs over the town.

A winter morning high above the district once called Alma, E. Hector Kyme's dog Robbie poses in an area recently landscaped by the town council. Sheffield Road curves past the former Lucas's 'Tilt' works and the Greyhound Inn. The open space immediately beyond the public house is the site of the former Silcock's works, where the axe used to execute King Charles I in 1649 was supposedly made.

Brightness after rain: a very early photograph by E. Hector Kyme showing Snape Hill Lane and Redfearn's shop at the junction with Princess Road in pre-war days.

A cloudy sundown near The Pines, above Snape Hill Lane, before the Second World War. The distant skyline tree between the Lombardy poplar trunks is one of the fine specimens on the Finney Fields, lost with the construction of the Unstone–Dronfield bypass in the early 1970s.

Hospital Sunday Parade along Eckington Road, Coal Aston, 1910.

Aston End stands at the very top of Green Lane, at its junction with Cross Lane. This low-built Tudor house still contains two pairs of cruck timbers; part of one set of crucks can be seen here in the parlour when Seymour Shepley and his family were living here, before 1962. This delightful old house with its yard and enclosing farm buildings is a rare remnant in a sea of modern development.

Coal Aston pond, 1950s. As with so many village ponds this one at the junction of Eckington Road and Drury Lane has long since disappeared, replaced by a boring corner of grass. Holmesfield's village pond survived longer, but has now vanished too.

The presentation of prizes won by members of the 4th Derbyshire Battalion Home Guard Rifle Club during 1946 took place at the White Swan Inn, Dronfield, on 20 December 1946. Left to right: Lt Col. G. Marples, F/Sgt F. Bentley, Supt. J. Brailsford, Robert Pearce, Capt. A. Cook, S.A. Thrussell (being presented with the County Challenge Cup), -?-, Capt. H. Grainger, Don Fisher, Capt. F.M. Gambles, Maj. A.L. Redfern, Col. E.M. Brooke Taylor (presenting cup), Maj. A.G. Wesley.

'Company Derbyshire Battalion Home Guards at Mosborough Hall, 1944. Third row, left to right: Phil Froggatt, ?. Goodall, -?-, -?-, Don Fisher, -?-, Bernard Wilson, ? McKinley, -?-, -?-, -?-, -?-. Second row: Arnold Dunham, -?-, -?-, Robert Pearce, -?-, -?-, -?-, -?-, -?-, -?-, Alf Collis, -?-, -?-, -?-, ?Biggin, -?-, -?-, -?-. Front row: -?-, A. Cook, Robinson, A. Wesley, Lt. Col. G. Marples, Capt. H. Grainger, Maj. A.L. Redfern, -?-, S.A. Thrussell, Capt. H. Gambles.

Doctor George Clifton writes a prescription in his surgery at The Hall, High Street, 1950. He joined Doctor Fletcher in the 1920s and later set up his own practice in High Street. His last home was Stubley Gate at the junction of Wreakes Lane and Stubley Lane, which was demolished to make a factory car park in about 1970.

Mrs Silcock, wife of John Walter Silcock and mother-in-law of E. Hector Kyme, makes a fine subject for a portrait created in the late 1940s and fittingly entitled 'Dignity'.

Marjorie Rooth (née Wood) was the first headteacher of the Ethel Lenthall Infants School, Marsh Avenue. Here she follows the explanations of Kim Bush one day in the early 1970s.

Barbara Ward Mathews was a most gifted actress and a leading light of the Dronfield Players Amateur Dramatic Society for many years. Here we see her in *Pink String and Sealing Wax*, produced in 1949.

A native of Dronfield who still lives in the town, David Ward showed early promise as a cricketer and joined the Derbyshire county team in 1966. He was a fast bowler and played for England in five Test matches. David last played for Derbyshire in 1976, having taken 348 first class wickets, but his career was ended by serious back injury.

ir Eric Mensforth and his wife lived at Lees Common,
arlow, during the 1960s and 1970s where they
ourned, drained, rebuilt drystone walls and planted
ver 20,000 trees'. In 1968 the National Trust
ccepted the Mensforths' gift of perpetual covenant to
reserve 31 acres of pasture and woodlands here at
ees Common. Sir Eric (born 1906), an experienced
lountaineer and eminent engineer, was President of
ne Westland Aircraft Company, Deputy Chairman of
ohn Brown & Co. Ltd and Master Cutler (1965–6).
e now lives in the south of England.

Self-portrait of the district's most celebrated
photographer and creator of many of the images in
this book. E. Hector Kyme (1906–87) took this
picture of himself in his garden at Cecil Road in 1974.

Members of the Baptist Chapel Sunday School about to undertake a Saturday collection for Dr Barnardo's Children's Homes, *c.* 1900. It is most unlikely that anyone seen here is alive today.

This photograph of Gosforth Lane couldn't be taken these days. The viewpoint is the Wainwrights' house, looking across the lane with G.N. Woodhead's Friesian herd leaving Manor Farm after morning milking, *c.* 1950. On the right is the garden hedge of Manor Croft. The foreground is now occupied by retirement homes and Beechwood Road takes up the sunlit space beyond.

A pair of photographs taken in Woodhead's fields beside Gosforth Lane from a spot close to the northern end of the Unstone–Dronfield bypass viaduct, probably 1928. Above: Manor Croft (built 1906) is clearly visible (right). Below: George Woodhead rides the binder in a field of wheat behind the cottages (left) which still exist.

Dronfield from the Finney Fields, *c.* 1900, looking north-east from the former Black Death or Cholera burial ground of 1832. Many of the town's old buildings are readily identified, and though lower Cecil Road and Hartington Road are already developed Coal Aston remains a quite separate village on its wooded hilltop far away.

Looking across the beautiful Gosforth Valley from the Finney Fields, summer 1964. Dronfield Woodhouse stands near the far horizon (left). Most of these fertile fields were shared by Manor Farm, High Street, and the twin Oxclose Farms. All has now vanished under the bricks and concrete of what was once claimed to be Europe's largest private housing estate, though some of the group of trees (left centre) still occupy a former pit bank behind Pentland Road shops.

Nearby, on the crest of the ridge and looking south over the wooded declivities of the Cowley district, stands Hills Farm, formerly home of the Timperleys and more recently the Binghams. Arnold Bingham was a well-known threshing contractor. This picture, taken in the mid-1960s, shows the early twentieth-century extension to the much earlier house – now entirely rebuilt.

Gosforth Colliery stood in the fields due west of the old town centre, beyond the last houses beside Gosforth Lane. It was known locally as 'Sheard's Pit' on account of its former owner. The site is now occupied by properties on Sheard's Drive. The old winding house and coke ovens were a playground for generations of children until 1965.

August sunset in the Gosforth Valley, *c.* 1952. G.N. Woodhead's Standard Fordson hauls the binder through a cornfield near 'Sheard's Pit'. Jim Ratcliffe is the driver and Maurice King operates the binder. On the following day a team of local women, including Joyce Ratcliffe, Elsie Ratcliffe and Mrs Bennett, would set about the tedious job of stooking the sheaves.

Work starts on the Unstone–Dronfield bypass, 29 July 1973. A bulldozer removes topsoil from the ridge adjacent to Cowley Lane, a short distance west of the Hyde Park Inn. This particular effort soon transformed Fisher's pasture field into a deep cutting.

The coming of the Unstone–Dronfield bypass changed some areas of the district out of all recognition. This photograph, for instance, shows Stubley Hollow in about 1958, looking up the hill towards the riding stables. The trees (right) hide the gable end of the cottages that still stand, but the bypass viaduct now rears above the spot where the photographer stood.

The top of Carr Lane, looking towards Dronfield, 1948. The lovely old buildings at Pool Farm (left) have been swept away and replaced with boring villas but the farmhouse remains. A photographer standing here today would take his life in his hands!

Dronfield Woodhouse Hall, *c.* 1900. This is one of the oldest properties in the district, the core of which dates from the fourteenth century. At its heart is the remaining set of cruck timbers – it is likely to have originally had at least five such sets. Sir Robert Barley lived here in the fifteenth century. He died in about 1470 and his tomb-effigy still stands in the parish church.

Obviously much altered over the centuries, the ancient house appeared in need of loving care and attention when the photograph above was taken. By 1968 the Smith family had done much to put this right (below).

CHAPTER TWO

HOLMESFIELD

Cartledge hamlet occupies a remarkable site next to an ancient defensive mound in Holmesfield. The outstanding building here is Cartledge Hall, built in 1493, probably to replace the original Hall built with five or more sets of cruck timbers, which is now the nearby barn, with only two sets of crucks remaining. Cartledge was the home of the wealthy Wolstenholmes from the mid-fifteenth century. John Wolstenholme (1562–1639) helped finance Henry Hudson's search for the North-West Passage in 1607–10 and the later effort by Baffin. The Hall was the home of the novelist Robert Murray Gilchrist up to his death in 1917, and his last surviving sister didn't leave until the end of the Second World War. Luckily for the old house it was rescued from dilapidation soon afterwards by the Sheffield industrialist Basil Doncaster, and was fully restored.

The adjacent Cartledge Grange was a 'grange' or outlying farm of Beauchief Abbey, and when some of the original cruck timbers were taken out of Cartledge Hall (now the barn) they were re-used here to join the oldest part (left) to what was formerly a separate kitchen (right). When this photograph was taken in about 1900 Cartledge Grange was still a working farm, and remained so throughout the twentieth century.

Woodthorpe Farm stands beside ancient Fanshawe Gate Lane between Lidgate and Totley in the parish of Holmesfield. It is older than Woodthorpe Hall, seen here, which stands opposite. This large house was either enlarged or built entirely using material from nearby Fanshawe Gate Hall, when that building was greatly reduced in the early seventeenth century. When this photograph was taken in about 1900 Woodthorpe Hall was farmed by the Wings; since that time it has been the family home of the Shepleys.

The old dovecote at Fanshawe Gate Hall, also in Holmesfield parish. Occupied by the powerful Fanshawe family from at least the fourteenth century, the old hall was much reduced in the early seventeenth century, probably when this grand garden adornment was constructed.

Cordwell Farm stands beside the road through Cordwell Valley, marked by a set of stone mounting steps on th
grass verge. In 1330 this hamlet was Caldwall, a name evolved from 'cald waella' – literally cold stream or sprin
Certainly leather was tanned in the district for a long period. Mrs Mabel Key of Cordwell Farm used t
accommodate guests visiting Edward Carpenter of Millthorpe, among them Captain Oates before he died with Sco
in Antarctica in 1912.

Billy Helliwell thatching a corn stack at Horsleygate Farm, Holmesfield, early 1970s. Such an activity was already long out of date, but the Wilsons continued to thresh their corn crops in the traditional way. The Helliwells were a large family of countrymen, including gifted craftworkers and poets, who originated from the lofty situation of Bank Green Farm, Fox Lane.

Alfred Lowe scything round the edge of the Over Field above Horsleygate Old Hall, *c.* 1928. The Lowes were a very old Holmesfield family, who lived at Horsleygate until Alf's death in December 1965.

The author's father, Arthur Redfern, with a Dairy Shorthorn beside Fox Lane, 1928.

Horsleygate Hall, Holmesfield, is an early nineteenth-century house added to a much earlier, smaller farmhouse on the northern slopes of Cordwell Valley. Once the home of the Penistones, it became the property of Major William Wilson early in the twentieth century. Major Wilson's father (also William) of Beauchief Hall had already built the nearby Kennels for the Barlow Hunt.

Barlow Hunt Pony Club summer meeting at Horsleygate, 1938. Back row: Elsie Wilson (sixth from left), Alan Osborne (extreme right). Second row, left to right: Mrs Osborne, -?-, -?-, William Wilson junior, Edith Woodhead, Edward Woodhead. -?-. Seated: Anne Wilson, Jennifer Lucas, Cynthia Lucas, Mrs M. Wilson, Major William Wilson, Kenneth Haslam, -?-, Verna Haslam, Tom Jackson.

Little Chatsworth is a name that appears on quite old maps, probably a semi-derisory appellation given when this row of stone cottages was first built beside Millthorpe Lane, just below Cartledge hamlet.

A motorcycle combination (complete with wicker sidecar) stands at the bend of Millthorpe Lane below Berry Hill just prior to the First World War. Johnnygate Farm and Barlow Woodseats Hall lie in the middle distance, but much of this particular view is nowadays hidden by foreground trees.

The ford and footbridge at Millthorpe, *c.* 1910. The view is still similar today, though rather spoiled since the old corn mill was demolished in the 1960s and a rash of quite inappropriate 'suburban' dwellings were put up here, removing much of the sylvan magic.

Early autumn ploughing at Millthorpe, 1937. Cyril and Florrie Stables came to Mill Farm in 1927. Here Cyril has an al fresco lunch behind his team.

Thirty-three years later in another field, October 1970. Colin Biggin spins out another row of potatoes for the hand-pickers in the Great Lamb Croft at Cordwell Farm. This activity is as much a thing of the past today as horse ploughing.

The author's mother, Rachel Redfern, in a Morgan at the summit of Fox Lane, above Cordwell Valley, on a bright day in 1928.

CHAPTER THREE

BARLOW

Barlow Woodseats Hall is the only remaining mansion house in Barlow parish. Manorial tenure began with Ascoit Musard in 1086 and ownership passed through members of several powerful families, including the Earl of Shrewsbury (from 1593), Duke of Newcastle (from 1691) and Duke of Portland (from 1741). In 1813 the parish was exchanged and came to John Henry Manners, Duke of Rutland. With the great Rutland sale of land and property in 1920 Barlow Woodseats changed hands.
The great house overlooking Johnnygate Lane is seen here soon after 1900. It is today the home of the Milwards, and separated from its ancient cruck barn and farmland.

Older Barlow residents will remember this lovely Tudor cottage beside Far Lane, next to Far Lane Farm and Yew Tree Farm. In its last years it was the home of Mrs Johnson who had a shop here in her living room. Customers remember going down steps from the lane to buy their bread and sweets. Sadly the local authority saw fit to demolish it in 1962. The poignant sight of honesty and bluebells each year is all that remains to remind us of this bit of old Barlow.

The author's Aunt Mary and grandfather, Reuben Dearden, on the footbridge in the bottom of Peakley Hill Wood, just below Dobbin Lane, summer 1926. Happily this place remains much as it was over seventy years ago.

On the Galloping Close (the Red Lane), near Lea Bridge over the Barlow Brook, a summer outing in 1921. Photographed are the author's Aunt Mary (left), grandfather Reuben Dearden, Aunt Joan (standing), cousin Herbert Rhodes (who became a famous golf professional) and mother Rachel (right).

The Barlow Brook in spate after two days of torrential rain in July 1973 when this part of Derbyshire received almost 7 inches of rain (equal to that normally expected in twelve summer weeks). This wall of water swept through Monk Wood Farm and threatened to drown the dairy herd while they were being milked.

Keeper's Cottage above Lea Bridge.
Until the early 1970s this delightful
hidden cottage was the home of
Major Wilson's gamekeepers. The last
incumbent was Mr Milton. Since that
time it has been much modified and
enlarged, and has lost most of its
former simple charm.

Miss Winifred Wilson (1881–1973) came to Highlightley Farm near Brindwoodgate in 1934, after the death of her mother at Beauchief Hall. A fine horsewoman, she hunted with the Barlow for eighty seasons and was a talented artist, a pupil of Sir John Arnesby Brown RA. She is seen here on her hunter Whitgift in March 1936.

Geoffrey Weston competing in the Holmesfield and Barlow Ploughing Association's match at Barlow, 1948.

The Barlow Hounds hunting along the edge of Monk Wood, *c.* 1946: Elsie Wilson (right), Huntsman Bill Spry and Anne Wilson.

A crafty nibble: haymaking at Bradley Lane Farm, Barlow, summer 1944. Brian Haslam is cocking hay.

Highlight of the summer season at Hackney Lane, Barlow, c. 1906. This is the annual well dressing celebration in August. We are standing at the bottom of Wilkin Mill and looking beyond the crowd to the old cottage which was swept away in the unenlightened 1960s.

Looking up Wilkin Hill before the First World War. Most of the old buildings seen here still exist in modified form. The thatched roof of The Cottage (beside the distant tree) has long since been replaced by slates and Miss Tetlow's cottage at the top of the hill was pulled down after the Second World War. Miss Tetlow was a former schoolteacher who died in 1924.

The Pinfold at Newgate, Barlow. Stray farm animals were impounded here until the offending farmer paid a fine. At the beginning of the Second World War eager local officials had the carved name 'Barlow' chiselled out of the lintel. No helping the invading enemy here!

The parish church of St Laurence is essentially a Norman church, so it was natural that when a chancel wa
added in 1867 it was in a neo-Norman style. This is one of the most attractive little churches in north Derbyshir
Its transeptal south chapel contains the tombs of the Barleys (Barlows), including that of Robert Barley (die
1467) and his wife. A later Barley became Bess of Hardwick's first husband.

Hackney House and garage, Barlow, early 1960s. Once a grocer's shop and blacksmith's workshop, this has now evolved into the popular Hackney House Restaurant and Tearoom, antique shop and interior design shop.

Nesfield, Barlow, is also known as Engine Hollow on account of the colliery railway line that carried coal from small pits here to Sheepbridge works. The railway has gone but these cottages remain. They are seen here with Grandfather Stevenson in his garden, c. 1900.

ACKNOWLEDGEMENTS

The author expresses his thanks to the family of the late E. Hector Kyme for permission to use eighty-six of his own photographs or from his collection, without which this book could not have been published. He also thanks Joyce Bennett, Dennis Clarebrough and the Old Dronfield Society, Wendy Crevel, Mary Crookes, Margaret Dixon, the late Mary Fearn, Frank Fisher, Eddy Gorman, Mrs D.V. Hague, Verna Haslam, Margaret Holman, Mr D. Ibbotson, the late Mrs Johnson, Russell Long, Sir Eric Mensforth, Christopher Nicholson, the late David Pearce, Steven Sampson, Sheila Simmonite, Shirley Stevenson, Raymond Temple and Anne Wilson for their generosity in the loan of photographs and, in some cases, help in identifying people and dates.

BRITAIN IN OLD PHOTOGRAPHS

SUTTON'S PHOTOGRAPHIC HISTORY OF TRANSPORT

To order any of these titles please telephone our distributor, Littlehampton Book Services on 01903 828800
For a catalogue of these and our other titles please ring Emma Leitch on 01453 731114